© Aladdin Books Ltd

Designed and produced by
Aladdin Books Ltd
70 Old Compton St
London W1

First published in
Great Britain in 1985 by
Franklin Watts
12a Golden Square
London W1

ISBN 086313 3096

Printed in Belgium

665.
M000246

The cover photograph shows
an oil refinery in the UK.

Photographic credits:
Cover Shell; pages 4/5 and 14, Zefa, pages 7
and 10, ESSO; pages 8, 12/13 and 17, Elf;
pages 18/19 and 22/23, Frank Spooner; page
21, Shell.

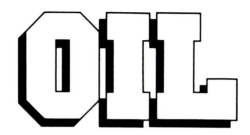

NIGEL HAWKES

Illustrated by
Ron Hayward Associates

Consultant
Stewart Boyle

Franklin Watts / Aladdin Books
London : New York : Toronto : Sydney

Introduction

Our lives depend on energy. We need it to heat and light our schools, homes and workplaces, and to fuel our cars, trains and aircraft. Industries need energy to make their products. Most of our energy currently comes from the "fossil" fuels: coal, gas and oil. Oil is the most important, because it provides the petrol for our transport.

The search for oil goes on all the time. We chase after its hidden riches on land, at sea, beneath deserts and in the frozen polar wastes.

Drilling for oil on the Gulf of Mexico, USA

Contents

Energy from oil

Oil is one of the best sources of energy because it can be used in many different ways. Like coal, it can be burned to make electricity. Like gas – which is often found with oil – it can provide heat.

But we can also make hundreds of different products from oil – glues, paints, plastics, dyes, detergents, nylon and foam cushions are just a few of them.

Oil is so important to us we are now drilling for it in the most difficult places. Amazing technology has been invented to do this – like the giant oil production platform in the photograph, which is being towed out to drill in the North Sea's Brent field.

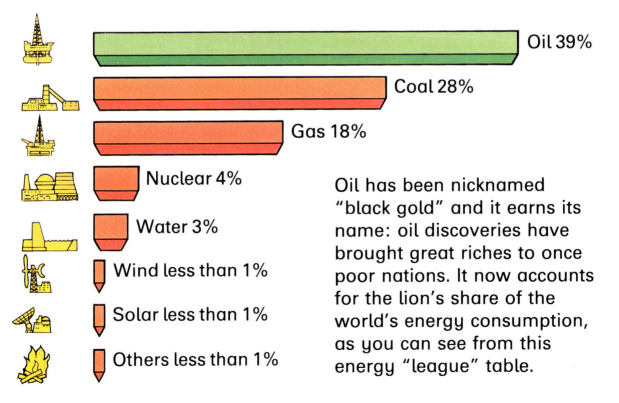

Oil 39%

Coal 28%

Gas 18%

Nuclear 4%

Water 3%

Wind less than 1%

Solar less than 1%

Others less than 1%

Oil has been nicknamed "black gold" and it earns its name: oil discoveries have brought great riches to once poor nations. It now accounts for the lion's share of the world's energy consumption, as you can see from this energy "league" table.

Finding it

Oil lies deep beneath the ground where it has been trapped under layers of rock. How do we know where to search for these oil reserves?

One method is to use a "seismic thumper", shown in the photograph. It carries a massive weight which sends shock waves through the earth when dropped to the ground. Echoes from the shock waves bouncing back off the layers of rock below show if oil may be present.

Sounding the desert floor in Saudi Arabia

Explosives can also be used to make shock waves. When oil exploration is taking place at sea, two special ships are used. One fires a water gun which sets off an explosion. The other tows a cable – which can be up to two km (one and a quarter miles) long – fitted with listening devices called hydrophones.

But the only way to make absolutely certain if oil is present is to drill a well.

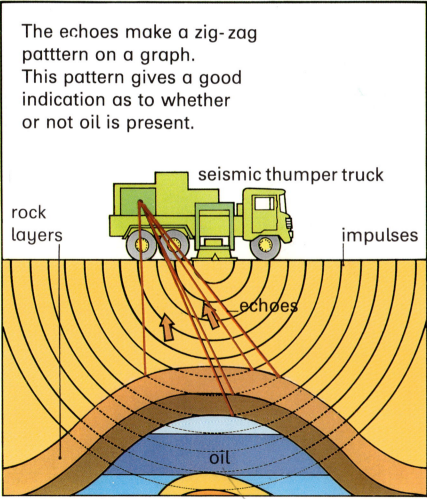

The echoes make a zig-zag patttern on a graph.
This pattern gives a good indication as to whether or not oil is present.

seismic thumper truck

rock layers

impulses

echoes

oil

Drilling for oil

Test drilling for oil is tough. The crew are based on an exploration rig where they work night and day. High above them, the drill hangs from a massive tower called a "derrick".

The drill is turned by a powerful engine. As it is lowered into the rock, sections of pipe are added to make it long enough to reach the oil far below. Sometimes the rock is so hard it takes an hour to drill a few centimetres. When the drill tip – the "bit" – gets blunt, the pipe is pulled up. It is taken apart, the bit is replaced, and then it is lowered once again.

Changing the drill bit

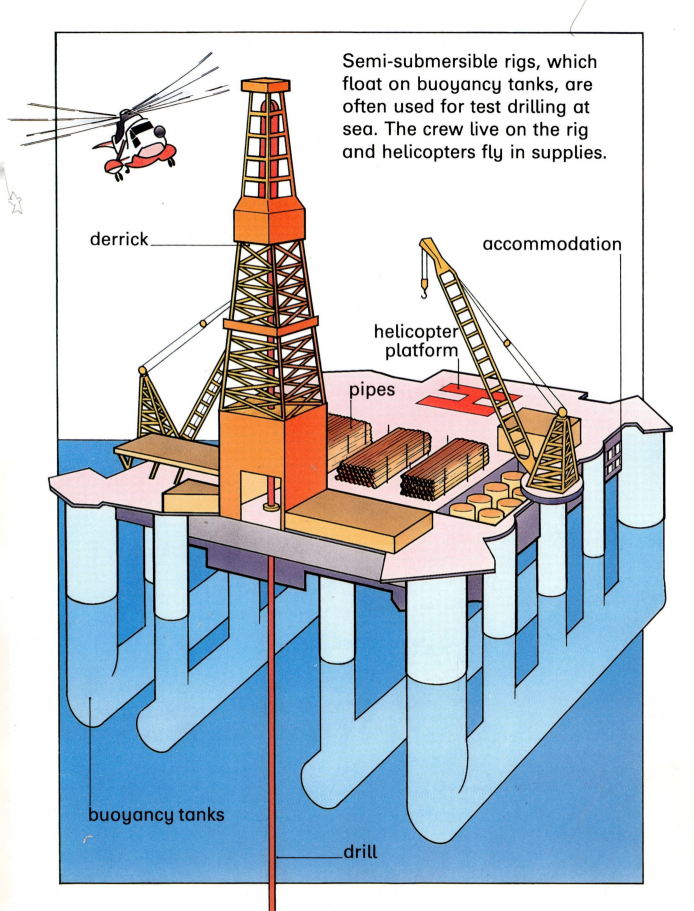

Semi-submersible rigs, which float on buoyancy tanks, are often used for test drilling at sea. The crew live on the rig and helicopters fly in supplies.

derrick

accommodation

helicopter platform

pipes

buoyancy tanks

drill

Production

Once oil is struck, it has to be pumped out of the ground. Production platforms are set up and wells are drilled over the whole field.

Ekofisk was the first oilfield to be developed in the North Sea. Engineers working from tugs and barges braved the stormy conditions to assemble all the vital equipment.

The complex has a vast tank which can hold a million barrels of oil, and two pipelines. One takes oil to England; the other takes gas to West Germany.

Part of the Ekofisk complex

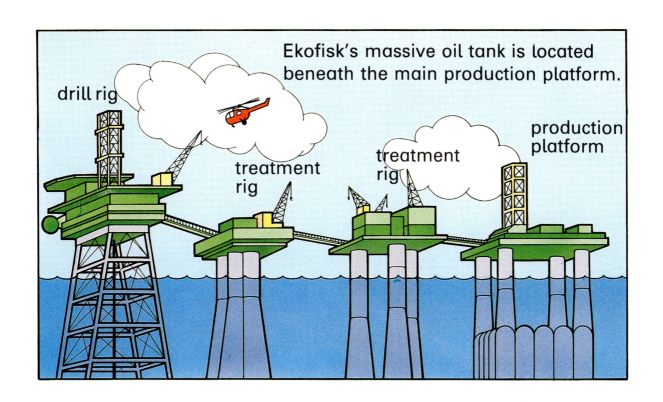

drill rig

Ekofisk's massive oil tank is located beneath the main production platform.

treatment rig

treatment rig

production platform

Alaskan pipeline

Pipeline

Pipelines carry their precious cargo of oil over land and under the sea. When oil was discovered in Alaska, a 1,300km (800 mile) pipeline was built. Crossing three mountain ranges and many rivers, across frozen earth called "permafrost", the oil has to be heated to keep it moving along.

For more than half its length it is raised on supports – as the photograph shows. The earth around the supports must always stay frozen, otherwise it turns to liquid mud. So the pipeline supports contain ammonia; this "vaporizes" if the ground warms up. It rises in the form of a gas; when meeting the cold air it cools and flows back down, keeping the ground frozen and the pipeline secure.

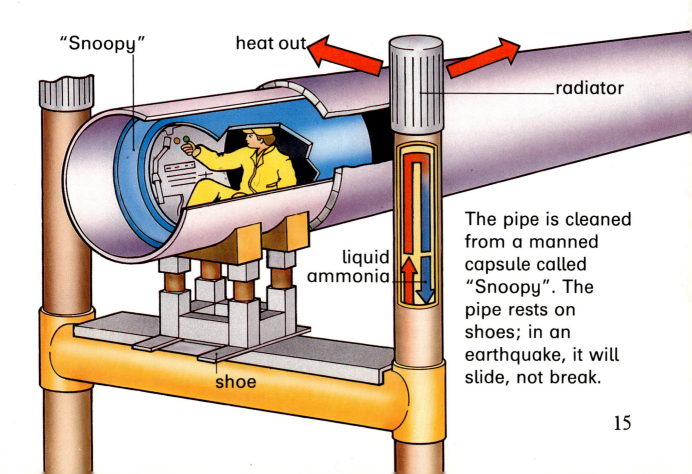

"Snoopy"

heat out

radiator

liquid ammonia

shoe

The pipe is cleaned from a manned capsule called "Snoopy". The pipe rests on shoes; in an earthquake, it will slide, not break.

15

At the refinery

Oil comes out of the ground in the form of a thick black liquid called "crude", which must be separated out to be useful. The photograph shows an oil refinery, which is where this separation takes place.

The crude is boiled and funnelled into a tall column. Vapour rises up the column and begins to change to liquid again, like steam on a cold window. The different liquids become fluid at different levels in the column.

The most valuable product is petrol; to get as much of it as possible the heavier liquids are split again, in a "catalytic cracker".

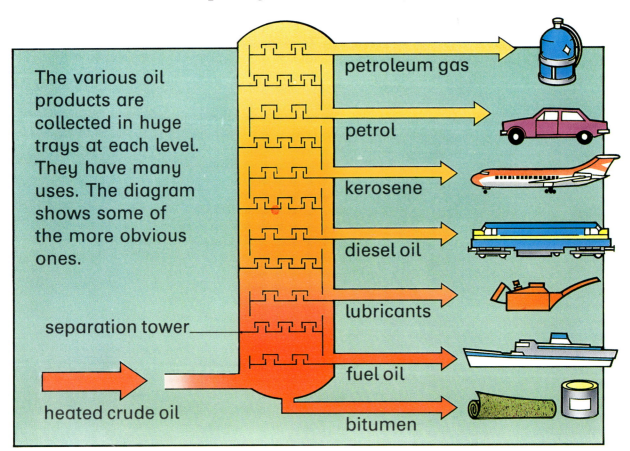

The various oil products are collected in huge trays at each level. They have many uses. The diagram shows some of the more obvious ones.

petroleum gas

petrol

kerosene

diesel oil

lubricants

separation tower

fuel oil

heated crude oil

bitumen

Problems

Everything in the oil industry is big, including the accidents. Sometimes oil wells can run out of control, spilling oil and causing fires. One such "blow-out" on a platform in a Mexican offshore oilfield burned for months and contaminated coasts far away in Texas.

Today's oil tankers carry up to 300,000 tonnes (295,245 tons), so when one is wrecked the spillage is colossal. The tanker shown below caught fire off South Africa.

Smoke billows from the burning tanker

Blow-out!

If action is not taken when a blow-out happens, the oil will burn for years. To put it out, the fire has first to be drenched with water.

Then, a drum of high-explosive is edged towards it. Hopefully, the sheer violence of the explosion will blow the fire out.

After oil?

The world is heavily dependent on oil. This is illustrated by the many cars on our roads, and the fuss caused by rising petrol prices.

1973 was the year of the "energy crisis" when oil prices shot up. Although prices have now fallen, the world economy has never fully recovered. Even more important is the fact that oil reserves will run out one day, and then we will have to manage without it.

Oil powered . . .

This will be very difficult. Cars, for example, not only need oil for fuel, but many of the parts inside are made from oil-based products. The steering wheel, the gear lever and the dashboard are all plastic, while the seats are made from nylon and foam.

While we may drive electric cars in the future, we will probably never find another energy source which is as versatile as oil.

. . . oil-based

Looking elsewhere

In the last 50 years we have used up nearly 40 per cent of the world's known oil and gas reserves. Because demand is constantly growing, and the developing countries are also using more oil, we have to look for new reserves.

A possible source lies in the oil shales of Colorado, and the tar sands of Alberta and Venezuela. Oil shales are a type of rock containing oil; tar sands contain oil and sand.

Mining the tar sand in Alberta

Why haven't these sources been used more? The problem is not separating the oil, which is not too difficult, but handling the volumes of material that have to be mined and treated. The waste from an oil shale plant would cover a football field to a height of 30 metres (100 feet) – every day!

However, one tar sand plant is operating in Alberta. It uses huge draglines to mine the sand, and turns out 130,000 barrels of oil a day.

Fact file 1

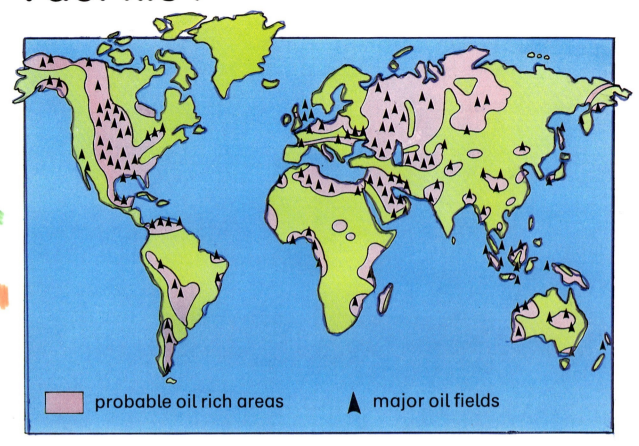

probable oil rich areas · major oil fields

The map above shows the world's oilfields. The countries of the Middle East have the largest share of the oil: more than 50% of known reserves are located there.

Why is it that some countries have oil, while others have none? The answer is that they contain the sites of oceans that covered the world's surfaces 300 million years ago.

non-porous rock

gas

oil

water

porous rock

These oceans teemed with masses of tiny plants and animals; it is from their remains that oil – and gas – are formed. Both seeped up through the porous rock but then got trapped beneath the layers of non-porous, or solid, rock in vast, underground lakes.

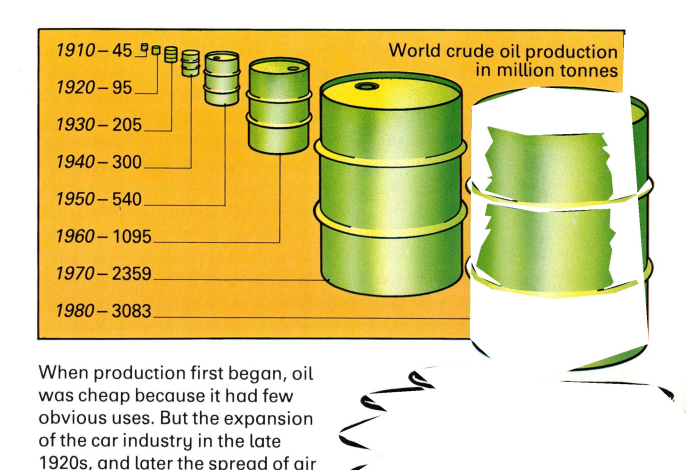

World crude oil production in million tonnes

Year	Production
1910	45
1920	95
1930	205
1940	300
1950	540
1960	1095
1970	2359
1980	3083

When production first began, oil was cheap because it had few obvious uses. But the expansion of the car industry in the late 1920s, and later the spread of air travel, meant that within a few decades oil had become one of the most valuable commodities ever known.

Oil makes some people very rich. The Sultan of Brunei, Sir Muda Hassanal Bolkiah, is said to earn £3,000 million a year from his country's oilfields!

The world's richest company is Exxon, one of the oil "giants". In 1982 it earned more than $97 billion from sales. Its income far outstrips the "gross national product" (GNP) of most African and South American countries.

The biggest oilfield in the world is the Ghawar field in Saudi Arabia. But the most dramatic *well* ever drilled was in 1901 at Spindletop, in Texas. It was a "gusher" that sprayed 800,000 barrels in nine days.

Oil consumption grew at a great rate in the 1950s and 1960s, but when prices rocketed it levelled off. Smaller cars, and better insulation in flats and houses have saved energy.

Fact file 2

The oil industry is moving into deeper water. The North Sea is rough, but not very deep, and platforms can stand safely on the seabed. But as the search moves to water more than 300 metres (980 feet) deep, narrow towers, fastened to the seabed by strong, steel "guy" ropes, are being used. Fortunately, deeper water is usually less choppy.

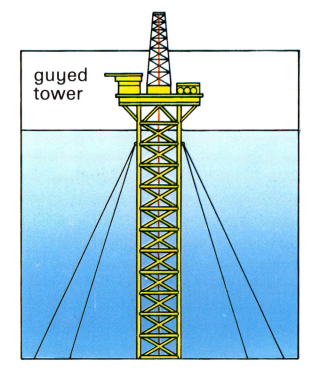
guyed tower

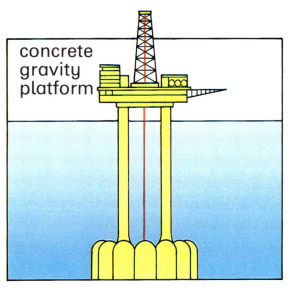
concrete gravity platform

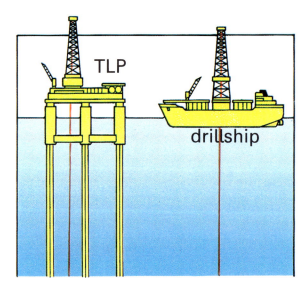
TLP

drillship

Conventional production platforms, like the concrete monsters used in the Brent Field, have the advantage that oil can be stored in the base to keep the pipelines full if production is interrupted. Sheer weight keeps the platform anchored to the sea bed. It can work in waters 200 metres (640 feet) deep.

A new platform has now been designed, suitable for depths up to 500 metres (1,640 feet). The Tension Leg Platform (TLP) floats, but is still anchored to the seabed by steel cables. In very deep water, drillships are used.

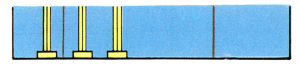

Many divers work in the industry: they inspect rigs, repair faults and check for geological movements of the seabed.

When production of oil in the North Sea began, hundreds of miles of pipeline were laid. Lengths of pipe were welded together on barges and were then lowered onto the seabed.

In the special "Big Jim" diving suit, it is possible to work at depths of 500 metres (1,600 feet). Sometimes divers work from small submarines called "submersibles".

As the search for oil takes the industry into deeper and deeper water, oil production "units" may one day be located on the seabed. The unit would handle 100,000 barrels of oil per day and would be powered by gas.

"Big Jim"

Concrete habitats, below, would be "home" for the workforce and all the vital equipment. The crew would remain underwater for many months at a time.

Air would be pumped from the surface, and the unit's lights could be raised and dimmed to give a sense of night and day.

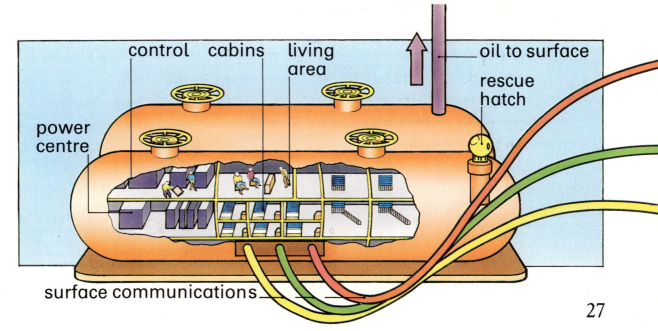

control   cabins   living area   oil to surface

rescue hatch

power centre

surface communications

Fact file 3

The countries with the greatest oil reserves are not always the top producers. And some producers want to save their oil resources and actually import some oil. Finally, large producers are sometimes also large consumers!

Major oil producing countries (figures in million tonnes for 1983)

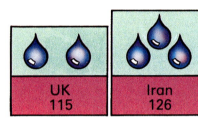

UK 115	Iran 126	Mexico 147	Saudi Arabia 260	USA 485	USSR 616

The UK is Europe's largest oil producer, thanks to the oilfields of the North Sea. And since these were discovered, smaller oilfields have also been found on shore.

Iran has huge oil reserves and was a major producer up to 1979. Since then, production has dropped, due to revolution at home and war with Iraq.

Mexico has found major new sources of oil in recent years and has consequently increased production. Much of Mexico's oil is exported by pipeline to the USA.

Saudi Arabia, with its huge oil reserves, could produce much more than it does. But it does not need the money. By keeping production low, oil prices are controlled.

The USA once supplied all its own oil needs, but in the 1970s it became a major importer of oil, buying from the Middle East and Canada.

The USSR is the world's biggest oil producer. This oil supplies its own vast energy needs, as well as those of Eastern Europe, Cuba and other countries in the Communist bloc.

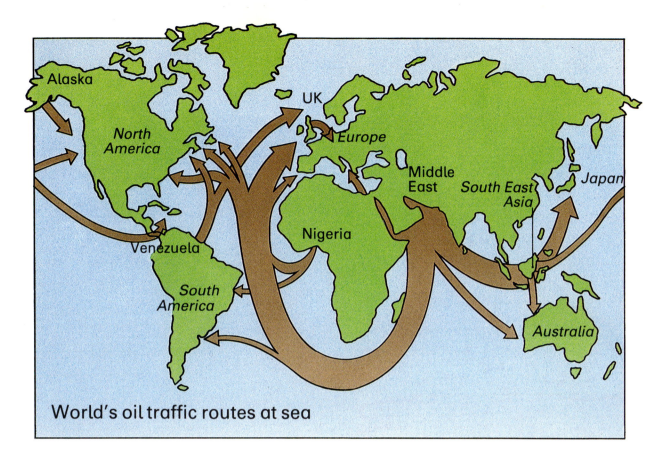

World's oil traffic routes at sea

The Middle East dominates the sea-borne oil trade, although its own production has fallen. "Supertankers" ply the oceans, carrying oil to most of the major consuming countries.

Japan, which has few natural resources of its own, is a major user of oil and imports more than 200 million tonnes each year. Most comes from Saudi Arabia, but 14% is supplied by the South East Asian oilfields.

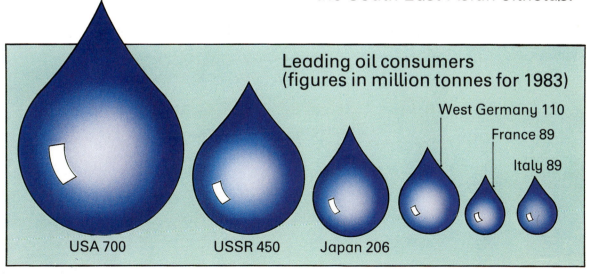

Leading oil consumers (figures in million tonnes for 1983)

West Germany 110
France 89
Italy 89

USA 700   USSR 450   Japan 206

Glossary

Ammonia   A chemical compound of nitrogen and hydrogen which boils to form a gas at low temperatures.

Barrel   A unit used to measure oil production. 1 barrel equals 159 litres (35 UK gallons, 42 US gallons). There are 7.3 barrels in a tonne, 6.6 barrels in a short US ton.

Bit   The cutting part of the drill. There are many different types; some are tipped with diamond for cutting into very hard rock.

Blow-out   An accident which occurs when an oil or gas well gets out of control and oil gushes out.

Catalytic cracker   The chemical process used in refineries to break down the heavier oils into the lighter, more valuable ones like petrol.

Gusher   When an exploration drill hits oil at high pressure and it sprays out (see Blow-out).

Mud   Chemical material (not real mud) pumped down a drill pipe to cool the bit and so prevent a blow-out.

Refinery   A chemical plant where crude oil is broken down into different liquids and gases.

Index

Acknowledgements
The publishers wish to thank the following
people and organizations who have helped
in the preparation of this book:
Friends of the Earth; Department of the
Environment UK; Conoco USA; Elf Petroleum
France; Enterprise Oil UK; Esso Petroleum UK;
Shell International.

Typeset by Dorchester Typesetting

PRINTED IN BELGIUM BY

INTERNATIONAL BOOK PRODUCTION